Everything I Need to Know

about

I Learne

Honor Books
Tulsa, Oklahoma

3rd Printing

Everything I Need to Know about Christmas I Learned from Jesus
ISBN 1-56292-552-0
Copyright 1998 © by Honor Books
P.O. Box 55388
Tulsa, Oklahoma 74155

Introduction

It's Christmas! A time of good cheer and holiday festivities, a time for singing carols and celebrating with family and friends. Twinkling lights, gaily wrapped presents, laughing children, jingling bells, hot wassail, fresh-cut pine—these are the sights and sounds and smells of Christmas!

Yet as the world celebrates the holiday, may the true meaning of Christmas never be lost. The birth of Jesus is our reason for the season. The Son of God came to give us hope and peace, to show us His Father's love and compassion for everyone.

Everything I Need to Know about Christmas I Learned from Jesus is all about seeing Jesus in every tradition, every celebration, and every moment of the Christmas season.

Joy to the world! The Lord has come!

Come to Bethlehem and see
Him Whose birth the angels sing;
Come, adore on bended knee
Christ the Lord, the new-born King.

Gloria in excelsis Deo!

Giving yourself is the greatest gift of all.

—◆—

Be imitators of God, therefore, as dearly loved children
and live a life of love,
just as Christ loved us and gave himself up for us.

Ephesians 5:1, 2 NIV

The African boy listened carefully as the teacher explained why people give presents to each other on Christmas Day. "The gift is an expression of our joy over the birth of Jesus and our friendship for each other," she said.

When Christmas Day came, the boy brought the teacher a sea shell of lustrous beauty. "Where did you ever find such a beautiful shell?" the teacher exclaimed. The youth named the spot, a bay several miles away. The teacher was touched. "Why . . . why, it's gorgeous . . . wonderful, but you shouldn't have gone all that way to get a gift for me."

His eyes brightening, the boy answered, "Long walk part of gift."

Despise not small beginnings.

———◆———

The time came for the baby to be born, and
she gave birth to her firstborn, a son. She wrapped
him in cloths and placed him in a manger,
because there was no room for them in the inn.

Luke 2:6, 7 NIV

He was born in an obscure village, the Child of a peasant woman. He grew up in another obscure village where He worked in a carpenter shop until He was thirty. Then for three years He was an itinerant preacher.

He never had a family or owned a home. He never set foot inside a big city. He never traveled 200 miles from the place He was born. He never wrote a book or held an office. He did none of the things that usually accompany greatness.

Nineteen centuries have come and gone, and today He is the central figure for much of the human race. All the armies that ever marched and all of the navies that ever sailed and all the parliaments that ever sat and all the kings that ever reigned, put together, have not affected the lives of man upon this earth as powerfully as this . . .

One Solitary Life.

It is Christmas every time you let
God love others through you . . .
every time you smile at your brother
and offer him your hand.

———◆———

Freely you have received, freely give.

Matthew 10:8 NIV

On a tour of duty in Vietnam an American soldier wandered through a village. It was Christmas and he whistled a Christmas carol as he strolled down a street. He was moved by the scores of children he saw. Dirty and hungry, many of the little ones in this war-torn country had little to rejoice over.

One tiny little girl shyly smiled as the soldier walked by. Her dress was ragged, her feet were bare, and her enormous brown eyes showed more sorrow and hardship than most adults have seen. He stopped and knelt in front of the little girl. He pulled a stick of chewing gum out of his pocket and held it out to her.

Her eyes welled up with tears and she turned away. Worried he had frightened or offended her in some way, he started to put the gum back in his pocket. But the little girl reached out and took it from his hand. She pointed to her eyes and spoke to him in broken English, "Happy tears, Mr. American, happy tears."

Love is a circle that goes on and on and on.

———•———

Give to everyone who asks you, and if anyone takes what belongs to you, do not demand it back. Do to others as you would have them do to you.

Luke 6:30, 31 NIV

*S*omehow not only for Christmas
But all the long year through,
The joy that you give to others
Is the joy that comes back to you.
And the more you spend in blessing
The poor and lonely and sad,
The more of your heart's possessing
Returns to make you glad.

Christmas began
in the heart of God.
It is complete only when it
reaches the heart of man.

———◆———

God . . . made his light shine in our hearts
to give us the light of the knowledge of the glory of God
in the face of Christ.

2 Corinthians 4:6 NIV

*U*ntil you feel the spirit of Christmas–
there is no Christmas.

All else is outward display–
so much tinsel and decoration.

For it isn't the holly, it isn't the snow.
It isn't the tree nor the firelight's glow.

It's the warmth that comes to the hearts of men
when the Christmas spirit returns again.[1]

*A*way in a manger, No crib for a bed,
The little Lord Jesus, Laid down His sweet head;
The stars in the sky Looked down where He lay,
The little Lord Jesus, Asleep on the hay.

The cattle are lowing; The Baby awakes,
But little Lord Jesus, No crying He makes;
I love Thee, Lord Jesus! Look down from the sky,
And stay by my cradle Till morning is nigh.

Be near me, Lord Jesus, I ask Thee to stay
Close by me forever, And love me, I pray;
Bless all the dear children In Thy tender care,
And fit us for heaven, To live with Thee there.

I am not alone at all.

————◆●◆————

"The virgin will be with child and will give birth to a son,
and they will call him Immanuel"
—which means, "God with us."

Matthew 1:23 NIV

God with us. That's what Immanuel means. The prophet Isaiah foretold Jesus' birth and said He would be called Immanuel and Wonderful Counselor, Mighty God, Everlasting Father, Prince of Peace.

No longer would we walk through life alone with God watching us from a distance. Jesus' birth, life, death, and resurrection eliminated the barrier of sin and death and brought God to us—and us to God.

In our darkest hours, in our saddest moments, when fear and violence and loneliness seem to rule the planet, let us take comfort that we are not alone. Immanuel. God with us.

Do all the good you can,
By all the means you can,
In all the ways you can,
In all the places you can,
At all the times you can!

———◆◆———

Love your enemies, do good to them.

Luke 6:35 NIV

One Christmas years ago, some townspeople wanted to share God's love in a practical way. They planted a vegetable garden beside the railroad tracks in a deserted area outside of town. The townspeople hoed, planted, and watered the garden until it produced a great harvest. They laid down their tools in the garden and went about their business, content to let nature take its course.

Over the next year, they planted nothing else and never picked a vegetable. But the garden grew and grew and grew, yet vegetables seldom rotted in the garden. Weeds were scarce, and the garden always seemed to have that "specially tended to" look.

Was it a miracle? Perhaps. An untold number of homeless hobos riding the railroads—perhaps dozens, perhaps hundreds—helped themselves to the crop and often spent many hours looking after the garden. For them, Christmas happened year-round, when they could always count on the blessing of good food—especially tasty as the fruit of their hard labors.

The circle of our Christmas associations and the lessons that they bring, expands! Let us welcome every one of them and summon them to take their place by the Christmas hearth.

The true light, which enlightens everyone,
was coming into the world.

John 1:9 NRSV

*E*verywhere, everywhere, Christmas tonight!

Christmas in lands of the fir tree and pine,
Christmas in lands of the palm tree and vine,
Christmas where snow peaks stand solemn and white,
Christmas where cornfields stand sunny and bright.

Christmas where children are hopeful and gay,
Christmas where old ones are patient and gray,
Christmas where peace, like a dove in its flight,
Broods o'er brave men in the thick of the fight.

Everywhere, everywhere, Christmas tonight!

For the Christ child who comes is the Master of all;
No palace too great, no cottage too small.[2]

Take Christ out of Christmas,
and December becomes
the bleakest and most colorless
month of the year.

*Today in the town of David a Savior has been
born to you; he is Christ the Lord.*

Luke 2:11 NIV

*S*o we will not "spend" Christmas . . .
nor "observe" Christmas.
We will "keep" Christmas—
keep it as it is . . .
in all the loveliness of its ancient traditions.
May we keep it in our hearts,
that we may be kept in its hope.

The means to gain happiness is
to throw out from oneself, like a spider,
in all directions an adhesive web of love,
and to catch in it all that comes.

———◆———

Love your neighbor as yourself.

Mark 12:31 NIV

Sometimes Sarah hated Christmas.

"Why do you let those strangers come here for dinner?" she whined to her mother. "They should eat at their own house!"

Sarah's mother hugged her daughter. "Let's go for a drive while the turkey cooks." In the car, they sang Christmas carols until they came to an area Sarah had never seen before.

"Why is that man sleeping on the sidewalk?" Sarah asked. Her mother slowed the car as Sarah stared at run-down buildings, piles of garbage, and barefoot children playing in an alley.

"This is where some people live," her mother replied.

"Outside? But it's cold!" Sarah looked down at her own warm coat and shoes. Her stomach growled, and she thought about Christmas dinner. "Are they hungry, too?" Her mother nodded. Sarah was quiet all the way home then locked herself in her room.

At dinner, Sarah hugged every "stranger" and presented a gift. Wrapped in pretty Christmas paper was every sheet, towel, blanket, shoe, hat, and mitten Sarah could find in the house.

Whatever else you give to your children,
give them roots and give them wings.

———◆———

Every year his parents went to Jerusalem
for the Feast of the Passover.
When he was twelve years old, they went up to the Feast,
according to the custom.

Luke 2:41, 42 NIV

The children could hardly wait to open presents. But wait they would. For every Christmas morning, their father shared a unique present that required them to take a family drive.

A friend of his had discovered and purchased a tract of land in the middle of the desert area they lived in. It had several natural springs that accented a rare desert wetland. He had turned it into a bird refuge.

The family visited just once a year, always on Christmas.

"Some things are so special that, if you did them everyday, you'd ruin them for sure," the father would say as the family huddled close to celebrate a tradition that became a cherished memory.[3]

The first noel the angel did say Was to certain
poor shepherds in fields as they lay;
In fields where they lay keeping their sheep
On a cold winter's night that was so deep.
They looked up and saw a star
Shining in the east, beyond them far;
And to the earth it gave great light,
And so it continued both day and night.
And by the light of that same star,
Three wise men came from country far;
To seek for a king was their intent,
And to follow the star wherever it went.

Then entered in those wise men three;
Full reverently upon their knee,
And offered there, in His presence,
Their gold and myrrh and frankincense.
Then let us all with one accord
Sing praises to our heavenly Lord,
That hath made heaven and earth of naught,
And with His blood mankind hath bought.

Noel, noel! Noel, noel!
Born is the King of Israel.

Nothing could be worse than the fear that one had given up too soon and left one unexplended effort which might have saved the world.

For to us a child is born, to us a son is given, and the government will be on his shoulders. And he will be called Wonderful Counselor, Mighty God, Everlasting Father, Prince of Peace. Of the increase of his government and peace there will be no end.

Isaiah 9:6, 7 NIV

32

Tell me the weight of a snowflake," a sparrow asked a wild dove. "Nothing more than nothing," was the answer.

"In that case, I must tell you a marvelous story," the sparrow said.

"I sat on the branch of a fir, close to its trunk, when it began to snow—not heavily, not in a raging blizzard—no, just like in a dream, without a sound, and without any violence. Since I did not have anything better to do, I counted the snowflakes settling on the twigs and needles of my branch. Their number was exactly 3,741,952. When the 3,741,953rd dropped onto the branch, nothing more than nothing, as you say, the branch broke off."

Having said that, the sparrow flew away.

The dove, since Noah's time an authority on the matter, thought about the story for awhile, and finally said to herself, "Perhaps only one person's voice is lacking for peace to come to the world."[4]

They are never alone who are accompanied by noble thoughts.

———◆———

Brothers, whatever is true, whatever is noble, whatever is right, whatever is pure, whatever is lovely, whatever is admirable—if anything is excellent or praiseworthy—think about such things.

Philippians 4:8 NIV

*S*o remember: while December
Brings the only Christmas day,
In the year let there be Christmas
In the things you do and say.

Wouldn't life be worth the living,
Wouldn't dreams be coming true,
If we kept the Christmas spirit
All the whole year through?[5]

It is good to be children sometimes, and never better than at Christmas, when the mighty Founder was a child Himself.

And the angel came to her and said,
"Greetings, favored one! The Lord is with you."

Luke 1:28 NRSV

*W*hen God wants
an important thing done in this world,
or a wrong righted,
He goes about it in a very singular way.

God does not release thunderbolts
or stir up an earthquake.

God simply has a tiny, helpless baby born,
perhaps in an obscure home,
perhaps of very humble parents.

Then He puts the idea into the parents' hearts,
they put it into the baby's mind,
and then—God waits.

The greatest good of every giving is—
when the giver is in the gift.

---

*Every good and perfect gift is from above,
coming down from the Father of the heavenly lights.*

James 1:17 NIV

*T*his is Christmas–the real meaning of it.
God loving, searching; giving Himself–to us.

Man's needing; receiving, giving himself–to God.
Redemption's glorious exchange of gifts!

Without which we cannot live;
Without which we cannot give to those we love
anything of lasting value.

This is the meaning of Christmas–
the wonder and the glory of it.

When I give, I give myself.

How much more will those who receive God's abundant provision of grace and of the gift of righteousness regain life through the one man, Jesus Christ.

Romans 5:17 NIV

S herry wanted a "real" oven for Christmas. But on Christmas morning, she could not believe her eyes. In front of her little *sister*'s stack of gifts was the oven. Sherry's gift was a miniature sewing machine, of all things! Her mother wanted to teach her to sew, but Sherry cried, making her mother feel terrible.

Eventually Sherry did sit with her mother and learn to sew, but the day was to come when her mother was no longer there. The hours they spent working together became some of Sherry's last good memories of their time together.

Our Father in heaven must look at us sadly as He implores us to enjoy the gifts He gives us. He knows what we need at the time. Sherry didn't know it then, but the best gift for her that Christmas was a sewing machine, because it meant precious time with her mother. For her, it was the best gift of all.

O come, o come, Emmanuel,
and ransom captive Israel,
That mourns in lonely exile here
until the Son of God appear.

O come, Thou Dayspring, come and cheer
our spirits by Thine advent here;
O drive away the shades of night
and pierce the clouds and bring us light.

Rejoice!
Rejoice!
Emmanuel shall come to thee,
O Israel.

Great as he was, Caesar Augustus
is now only an echo of ancient times,
while the name of the child he had never
heard of is spoken by millions
with reverence and love.

In those days a decree went out from Emperor Augustus
that all the world should be registered.

Luke 2:1 NRSV

The Palace and the Stable

*I*t was the seven hundred and fifty-third year
since the founding of Rome.
Gaius Julius Caesar Octavianus Augustus
was living in the palace of the Palatine Hill,
busily engaged upon the task of ruling his empire.
In a little village of distant Syria,
Mary, the wife of Joseph the carpenter,
was tending her little boy,
born in a stable of Bethlehem.

This is a strange world.
Before long, the palace and the stable
were to meet in open combat.
And the stable was to emerge victorious.

Joyful, all ye nations rise,
Join the triumph of the skies!

———◆———

He has brought down rulers from their thrones
but has lifted up the humble.

Luke 1:52 NIV

The last Christmas that was supposed to ever be celebrated in Cuba was in 1956. Fidel Castro outlawed any display of religion when he succeeded in his revolution.

But in 1997, almost half a century later, the same man allowed Christmas to be celebrated in preparation for Pope John Paul II's visit the following January.

Even after five decades of repression, millions of Cuban people embraced Christmas that year.

The love for the Christ Child had not been killed. For truth endures forever.[6]

You can never truly enjoy
Christmas until you can look
up into the Father's face and tell
him you have received his Christmas gift.

———◆———

If you know how to give good gifts to your children,
how much more will your Father in heaven
give good things to those who ask him!

Matthew 7:11 NRSV

I remember visiting my middle son's nursery school class, at the request of his teacher, so that I could observe a "problem child" in the class. It so happened that I was sitting and observing a group of boys, including my son, who sat in a circle nearby.

Their conversation went like this:

Child A: "My daddy is a doctor and he makes a lot of money and we have a swimming pool."

Child B: "My daddy is a lawyer and he flies to Washington and talks to the president."

Child C: "My daddy owns a company and we have our own airplane."

Then my son (with aplomb, of course): "My daddy is here!"

Children regard the public presence of their parents as a visible symbol of caring and connectedness that is far more significant than any material support could ever be.[7]

The great man is he who does not
lose his child's heart.

——◆——

As a father has compassion on his children, so the
Lord has compassion on those who fear him.

Psalm 103:13 NIV

Two boys couldn't wait for Christmas. They'd asked for trains, and there were hints they'd get them. On Christmas morning, they were up before dawn.

Sure enough, under the tree sat a gleaming passenger train for the younger boy and a sturdy freight for the older boy. They ran excitedly into their parents' bedroom, their eyes sparkling with delight. Mom said they were great. Dad showed honest but groggy interest. Another surprise stood in the basement: a huge table covered with track, wired so they could run both trains at the same time. They loved it!

The boys didn't know their dad had worked all night building, laying track, and wiring. They couldn't appreciate his hours of planning, expensive shopping, lost sleep; and the care needed for quiet construction.

But years later they would understand their father's sacrificial love when they, too, became fathers. What loving father's heart doesn't leap for joy at blessing his children?

Peace is our gift to each other.

———◆———

And suddenly there was with the angel a multitude
of the heavenly host, praising God and saying,
"Glory to God in the highest, and on earth peace
to all on whom his favor rests."

Luke 2:13, 14 NRSV

*O*n a winter night
When the moon is low
The rabbits hop
on the frozen snow.
The woodpecker sleeps
in his hole in the tree
And fast asleep
is the chickadee.
Twelve o'clock
And the world is still
As the Christmas star
comes over the hill.
The angels sing,
and sing again:
"Peace on earth,
goodwill to men."[8]

*H*ark! the herald angels sing, "Glory to the newborn King;
Peace on earth, and mercy mild–God and sinners reconciled!"
Joyful, all ye nations rise, join the triumph of the skies;
With the angelic hosts proclaim, "Christ is born in Bethlehem!"
Hark! the herald angels sing, "Glory to the newborn King!"

*C*hrist, by highest heaven adored, Christ, the everlasting Lord!
Late in time behold Him come, offspring of the virgin's womb.
Veiled in flesh the Godhead see; hail the incarnate Deity,
Pleased as man with men to dwell, Jesus, our Emmanuel.
Hark! the herald angels sing, "Glory to the newborn King!"

Hail the heaven born Prince of Peace!
Hail the Sun of Righteousness!
Light and life to all He brings,
risen with healing in His wings.
Mild He lays His glory by,
born that man no more may die,
Born to raise sons of the earth.
Born to give them second birth.

Hark! the herald angels sing,
"Glory to the newborn King!"

What does God look like?

———◆●◆———

Christ Jesus ... made himself nothing,
taking the very nature of a servant,
being made in human likeness.

Philippians 2:5, 7 NIV

*W*hat are you drawing?"
a mother asked her five-year-old.

"A picture of God," the little girl answered.

The mother responded,
"But no one knows what God looks like."

"They will when I get through," the little girl replied.[9]

We may seek God by our intellect, but we only can find him with our heart.

＊

No one has ever seen God.
It is God the only Son,
who is close to the Father's heart,
who has made him known.

John 1:18 NRSV

Almost nobody has seen God, and almost nobody has any real idea of what He is like.

The truth is, the idea of seeing God suddenly and standing in a very bright light is not necessarily a completely comforting and appealing idea.

But everyone has seen babies, and most people like them. If God wanted to be loved as well as feared he moved correctly here.

Christmas is either all falsehood or it is the truest thing in the world.[10]

The only gift is a portion of thyself.

And a little child will lead them.

Isaiah 11:6 NIV

During the Christmas season when my daughter was three years old, the number of presents under the tree slowly increased as the day approached.

Caught up in the spirit and excitement of gifts and giving as only three-year-olds can be, one morning she was picking up, examining, shaking, and guessing what was inside of every package. Then, in a burst of inspiration, she picked up a bow that had fallen off one present and held it on top of her head. She looked up with twinkling eyes and beamed a smile as bright as the Star as she said, "Look at me, Daddy! I'm a present!"

Her words were more true than she realized.[11]

The hinge of history
is on the door of a Bethlehem stable.

———◆———

The shepherds ... went with haste
and found Mary and Joseph,
and the child lying in the manger.

Luke 2:15, 16 NRSV

*T*here are some of us who think to ourselves,
"If I had only been there!
How quick I would have been to help the Baby.
I would have washed his linen.
How happy I would have been
to go with the shepherds
to see the Lord lying in the manger!"

We say that because we know how great Christ is.
But if we had been there at that time,
we would have done no better
than the people of Bethlehem.

We have Christ in our neighbor.
Why not serve Him now!

Love is that condition in which the happiness of another person is essential to your own.

But God showed his great love for us by sending Christ to die for us while we were still sinners.

Romans 5:8 TLB

One Christmas day, five-year-old Amy unwrapped a beautiful doll given to her by her grandmother.

"Oh, thank you, Grandma!" Amy squealed excitedly, hugging her new gift.

Amy played with her new doll for several hours, but toward the end of the day she brought out one of her old dolls. She cradled the tattered doll in her arms. It had lost much of its hair; its nose was broken; one eye was gone.

"Well, well," smiled Grandma. "I see you like this doll the best."

"I like the beautiful doll you gave me, Grandma," replied Amy.

"But I love this old doll the most, because if I didn't love her, no one else would."[12]

Every little child in all the world has
been a little safer since the coming
of the Child of Bethlehem.

———◆———

Then Herod ... was in a furious rage ...
and killed all the male children in Bethlehem.

Matthew 2:16 NRSV

*O*ur whole Roman world had gone dead in its heart
because it feared tragedy,
took flight from suffering,
and abhorred failure.

In fear of tragedy we worshipped power.

In fear of suffering, we worshipped security.

During the rising splendor of our thousand years,
we had grown cruel, practical, and sterile.

Rome did conquer the whole world,
but in the process we lost our souls.

What Child is this, who, laid to rest,
on Mary's lap is sleeping?
*Whom angels greet with anthems sweet,
while shepherds watch are keeping?*

Why lies He in such mean estate
where ox and ass are feeding?
*Good Christian, fear—for sinners here
the silent Word is pleading.*

So bring Him incense, gold and myrrh—
come, rich and poor, to own Him;
The King of kings salvation brings—
let loving hearts enthrone Him.

This, this is Christ the King,
whom shepherds guard and angels sing;
Haste, haste to bring Him laud—
the Babe, the Son of Mary.

Christmas is a spark that
ignites in someone's heart.

———◆———

Everyone must come, men, women and children.
And each new generation will listen and
learn to worship the LORD.

Deuteronomy 31:12 NAS

W hy do I do this?" the children's director asked herself after a pageant rehearsal that went badly. She thought back to a Christmas long ago when she was dressed as Mary with a dish towel wrapped around her head. Smiling, she recalled how she first felt her heart become tender and open to the Savior whose birth they celebrated. "I guess I do know why I do it," she sighed. "I just wish it were as simple as it was back then."

The night of the program came. Watching the children march onto the platform, she realized that Christmas is still simple. The music and set decorations may have grown more elaborate, but Christmas is still children gathered in a church singing about a Savior who was born on Christmas night.

And maybe, just maybe, through the music and the drama of a Christmas pageant at church, the children are feeling the first spark of Christmas in their hearts.

 How many angels are there?
One–who transforms
our life–is plenty.

---

*An angel of the Lord appeared to Joseph in a dream
and said, "Get up, take the child and his mother,
and flee to Egypt, and remain there until I tell you;
for Herod is about to search for the child, to destroy him."*

Matthew 2:13 NRSV

We so often hear the expression, "the voice of an angel," that I got to wondering what an angel would sound like. So I did some research. I discovered that an angel's voice sounds remarkably like a person saying, "Hurry up!"

An angel appears to Joseph in a dream, when Herod is slaughtering the infants, and says, "Go quickly!"

An angel says to Gideon, "Arise and go in this thy might."

An angel comes to Peter in jail and says, "Rise quickly."

An angel appears to Philip and says, "Arise and go."

Listen carefully and you can hear the voice of angels above the contemporary din, a voice that ought to get us out of lounge chairs and comfortable beds, saying, "Arise! Go quickly!"[13]

It is not even the beginning of Christmas until it is Christmas in your heart.

———◆———

The spirit of the Lord is upon me, because
he has anointed me to bring good news to the poor.
He has sent me to proclaim release to the captives and
recovery of sight to the blind, to let the oppressed
go free, to proclaim the year of the Lord's favor.

Luke 4:18, 19 NRSV

74

*W*hen the song of the angels is stilled,
When the star in the sky is gone,
When the kings and princes are home,
When the shepherds are back with their flock,

Then the work of Christmas begins:

To find the lost, to heal the broken;
To feed the hungry, to release the prisoner;
To rebuild the nations, to bring peace among enemies;
To make music in your heart.[14]

Interpersonal relationships are
the most valued and cherished gifts of all.
The Bible teaches that God gave a Person
as a gift to every one of us, and
that Person is Jesus Christ.

I am come that they may have life, and have it to the full.

John 10:10 NIV

*C*hristmas, my child, is love in action.

When you love someone,
you give to them,
as God gives to us.

The greatest gift He ever gave
was the Person of His Son,
sent to us in human form
so that we might know
what God the Father is really like!

Every time we love,
every time we give,
it's Christmas.[15]

Christmas is the season
for kindling the fire of hospitality
in the home, the genial flame of
charity in the heart.

———◆◆◆———

It is more blessed to give than to receive.

Acts 20:35 NIV

I have always thought of Christmas…
as a good time:
a kind, forgiving, charitable, pleasant time;
the only time I know of, in the long calendar of the year,
when men and women seem by one consent
to open their shut-up hearts freely.…

And though it has never put
a scrap of gold or silver in my pocket,
I believe that it has done me good,
and will do me good.

And so, as Tiny Tim said,
"A merry Christmas to us all;
God bless us, every one!"

I heard the bells on Christmas day
their old familiar carols play,
And wild and sweet the words repeat
of peace on earth, good will to men.

I thought how, as the day had come,
the belfries of all Christendom
Had rolled along the unbroken song
of peace on earth, good will to men.

*A*nd in despair I bowed my head:
"There is no peace on earth," I said;
"Hate is strong, and mocks the song
of peace on earth, good will to men."

Yet pealed the bells more loud and deep:
"God is not dead, nor doth He sleep;
The wrong shall fail, the right prevail,
with peace on earth, good will to men."

Then ringing, singing on its way,
the world revolved from night to day
A voice, a chime, a chant sublime
of peace on earth, good will to men!

Selfishness makes Christmas a burden;
Love makes it a delight.

*Love your enemies
and pray for those who persecute you,
so that you may be children
of your Father who is in heaven.*

Matthew 5:44, 45 NRSV

*P*eople are unreasonable, illogical, and self-centered.
Love them anyway.
If you do good, people will accuse you of selfish ulterior motives.
Do good anyway.
If you are successful, you will win false friends and true enemies.
Succeed anyway.
The kindness you do today will be forgotten tomorrow.
Be kind anyway.
The biggest people with the biggest ideas can be shot down
by the smallest people with the smallest minds.
Think big anyway.
People favor underdogs but follow only top dogs.
Fight for some underdogs anyway.
What you spend years building may be destroyed overnight.
Build anyway.

The joy of brightening a child's heart creates the magic of Christmas.

Whatever you did for one of the least of these brothers of mine, you did for me.

Matthew 25: 40 NIV

It's Christmas day in the southwest. Families are gathered to celebrate together.

But Mindy is at a shelter for neglected and homeless children. A chubby little boy, Sam, sits on her lap. They have just cleaned him up, and discovered bald patches on his head where someone has pulled his hair out.

At bedtime, Mindy cares for six children one by one, changing diapers, giving a bath if needed, and taking them to the nursery where soft music plays. She hugs each child and whispers, "I love you." She saves Sam, the newcomer, for last.

Within minutes he is asleep, safe, warm and loved on a Christmas night.[16]

The Word of God, Jesus Christ,
on account of his great love for us,
became what we are
in order to make us what he is.

He is the image of the invisible God.

Colossians 1:15 NIV

Norman A. McMurry tells about a palace in the city of Rome which has a great high dome. Inside that dome there is a painting known as *The Dawn* by Guido Reni.

In order that visitors may see this masterpiece, a table has been placed directly beneath the dome, and on the table a large mirror. When people look into the mirror, they see the majestic painting far above.

In a way this is what the Incarnation is all about. Jesus of Nazareth is the "mirror-image" of God.[17]

The best of all gifts around
any Christmas tree:
the presence of a happy family
all wrapped up in each other.

———◆———

Whoever welcomes one such child in my name welcomes
me, and . . . the one who sent me.

Mark 9:48 NRSV

One Christmas, a father gave his four-year-old daughter a colorful edition of *The Three Little Pigs*. Soon she acquired a fixation for her new gift and insisted that her daddy read it to her every night at bedtime.

The man eventually tired of the story, and came up with the idea of tape-recording it. The next night, when his daughter asked him to read, he showed her how to press the "Play" button.

This worked for a couple of nights, but then the little girl handed the storybook to her father.

"But honey," he said, "you know how to turn on the recorder."

"Yes," she said, "but I can't sit on its lap."[18]

This Jesus of Nazareth, without money and arms, conquered more millions than Alexander, Caesar, Mohammed, and Napoleon.

---◆---

Do not be afraid; for see—I am bringing you good news of great joy for all the people.

Luke 2:10 NRSV

*S*ome say that ever again
that season comes
wherein our Saviour's birth is celebrated
the bird of dawning
singeth all night long.

And then, they say,
no spirit dare stir abroad.
No planet strikes.
No fairy takes.
Nor witch hath power to charm.

So hallow'd and so gracious
is the time.

Now and then it's good to pause in our pursuit of happiness and just be happy.

———◆———

I am come that they might have life, and that they might have it more abundantly.

John 10:10 KJV

On Christmas Eve, a family dressed for church. Glowing tree lights, gaily wrapped gifts, seasonal smells, and the sounds of excited children warmed hearts as an icy wind howled outside.

The father sensed trouble when he turned the tap for shaving water. Nothing. "Frozen pipes!" he called to his wife. With hair dryer, extension cord, and flashlight in hand, he crawled through the attic. *It sure is cold in here*, he thought, knees and palms balanced on floor joists. A few minutes of hair dryer heat and insulation wrapping later, he emerged to begin a mad, get-ready dash for church.

In the warm loft of the old country sanctuary, he stood with his wife and the rest of the choir, bathed in the candlelight glow of "Silent Night," their hearts filled with joy somehow made sweeter by overcoming life's unexpected challenges.

Later at home he found a gift that let him sleep that night in heavenly peace: thawed, uncracked pipes.

Silent night! Holy night!
All is calm, all is bright
Round yon virgin mother and Child,
holy infant, so tender and mild
Sleep in heavenly peace,
sleep in heavenly peace.

Silent night! Holy night!
Shepherds quake at the sight;
Glories stream from heaven afar;
heavenly hosts sing alleluia
Christ the Savior is born!
Christ the Savior is born!

Silent night! Holy night!
Son of God, love's pure light
Radiant beams from Thy holy face
with the dawn of redeeming grace
Jesus, Lord at Thy birth,
Jesus, Lord at Thy birth.

The most important thing
a father can do for his children
is to love their mother.

———◆———

Joseph, son of David, do not be afraid
to take Mary as your wife, for the child conceived
in her is from the Holy Spirit.

Matthew 1:20 NRSV

*J*oseph dearest, Joseph mine
Help me rock this child of mine
Here mid sheep and friendly kind
We watch our babe in slumber softly dreaming.

Gladly, dearest Mary mine
I will rock this child of thine
While God's stars above us shine
Here love's pure light upon us all is streaming.

I never realized God's birth before,
How He grew likest God in being born . . .
Such ever was love's way–to rise, it stoops.

———◆———

Look, the Lamb of God,
who takes away the sin of the world!

John 1:29 NIV

The Lamb

*L*ittle lamb, who made thee? Dost thou know who made thee,
Gave thee life and bade thee feed By the stream and o'er the mead;

Gave thee clothing of delight, Softest clothing, woolly, bright;
Gave thee such a tender voice, Making all the vales rejoice?

Little lamb, who made thee? Dost thou know who made thee?
Little lamb, I'll tell thee; Little lamb, I'll tell thee.

He is called by thy name, For He calls Himself a Lamb;
He is meek and He is mild, He became a little child.

I a child and thou a lamb, We are called by His name.
Little lamb, God bless thee! Little lamb, God bless thee!

The stars stood at midnight,
And tame or wild, all creatures knelt
To worship the Child.

———◆———

The wolf also shall dwell with the lamb, and the leopard shall lie down with the kid; and the calf and the young lion together; and a little child shall lead them.

Isaiah 11:6 KJV

S itting in the front row of a Christmas Eve church service, he was ready to worship God and celebrate the coming of His Son.

But as he looked toward where the minister stood, there, right by the crèche was a frog. A frog at Christmas?!

At one point, he was certain the minister had stepped on the tiny amphibian. There appeared to be a stain on the carpet by his shoe. But just as the chorus of "It Came Upon A Midnight Clear" began, there was movement at the base of a poinsettia.

The creature resumed his watch by the manger scene, just as animals two centuries earlier had done.[19]

The only blind person at Christmas-time is he who has not Christmas in his heart.

———◆•◆•◆———

The blind receive sight, the lame walk, those who have leprosy are cured, the deaf hear, the dead are raised, and the good news is preached to the poor.

Luke 7:22 NIV

*R*eady for Christmas," she said with a sigh
As she gave a last touch to the gifts piled high . . .
Then wearily sat for a moment to read
Till soon, very soon, she was nodding her head.
Then quietly spoke a voice in her dream,
"Ready for Christmas, what do you mean?"
She woke with a start and cry of despair.
"There's so little time and I've still to prepare.
Oh Father! Forgive me, I see what You mean!
To be ready means more than a house swept clean.
Yes, more than the giving of gifts and a tree.
A heart that is free from bitterness and sin.
So be ready for Christmas—and ready for Him!"

O Come, Thou wisdom from on high, And order all things, far and nigh; To us the path of knowledge show, And cause us in her ways to go.

Wisdom ... is ... pure, peace-loving, considerate, submissive, full of mercy and good fruit, impartial and sincere.

James 3:17 NIV

Stories about the wise men have been repeated through the centuries since Jesus' birth. Some site twelve seekers, others six, some four, and many three since three gifts were given. The Bible narrative gives no exact number.

On their journey, they got lost, showed up at the wrong place, were late for Jesus' birth, and had to sneak home.

But incredibly, with only a star to guide them, they found Jesus. Wise men and women still do today.[20]

We three kings of Orient are,
bearing gifts we traverse afar,
Field and fountain, moor and mountain,
following yonder star.

Born a King on Bethlehem's plain,
gold I bring to crown Him again,
King forever,
ceasing never over us all to reign.

Frankincense to offer have I;
incense owns a Deity nigh;
Prayer and praising, all men raising,
worship Him, God on high.

*Myrrh is mine; its bitter perfume
breathes a life of gathering gloom:
Sorrowing, sighing, bleeding, dying,
sealed in the stone-cold tomb.*

*Glorious now behold Him arise,
King and God and Sacrifice;
Alleluia! Alleluia!
Earth to heaven replies.*

*O star of wonder, star of night,
star with royal beauty bright,
Westward leading, still proceeding,
guide us to Thy perfect light.*

Wise men still seek Him.

Now when Jesus was born in Bethlehem of Judaea in the days of Herod the king, behold, there came wise men from the east.

Matthew 2:1 KJV

An hour before the Christmas Eve pageant, the director was frantic. "Where are the three kings?" Dressed in their elegant costumes, the three youths had vanished.

"Well, they'll turn up," the costume coordinator said with a sigh, helping an angel with his wings.

Outside, the "three kings" walked laughing through falling snow, oblivious to the pageant panic they'd caused. A block away, they waited until no one was around, then knelt statue-like by the town's life-size manger scene. As drivers stopped to look, the "three kings" walked off into the night. After a repeat performance near the light-draped Christmas tree on Main Street, they arrived back at church just in time for the pageant, where they played their parts with new-found zeal.

One wintry night, three "wise guys" searched for fun. What they had found was a deeper connection to the birth of Jesus.

Sometimes we don't get
the things we want; but we get
the things we need.

***

There are different kinds of gifts, but the same spirit.

I Corinthians 12:4 NIV

A little girl who had recently become the big sister
of a new baby brother
listened to the story about the Wise Men's gifts
to the Baby Jesus.
She thought a moment and then said,
"Well, I guess gold and all that stuff are all right,
but I'll bet Mary really wished
somebody had brought some diapers."[21]

Seek joy in what you give
not in what you get.

———◆━●━◆———

When they saw that the star had stopped,
they were overwhelmed with joy. On entering the house,
they saw the child with Mary his mother; and
they knelt down and paid him homage.

Matthew 2:10, 11 NRSV

I am Gaspar. I have brought frankincense,
and I have come here to say that life is good.
That God exists. That love is everything.
I know it is so because of the heavenly star."

"I am Melchior. I have brought fragrant myrrh.
Yes, God exists. He is the light of day.
The white flower is rooted in the mud,
and all delights are tinged with melancholy."

"I am Balthazar. I have brought gold.
I assure you, God exists. He is great and strong.
I know it is so because of the perfect star
that shines so brightly in Death's diadem."

"Gaspar, Melchior, Balthasar: be still.
Love has triumphed, and bids you to its feast.
Christ, reborn, turns chaos into light,
and on His brow He wears the Crown of Life."

Adults are obsolete children.

O LORD, our LORD, how majestic is thy name in all the earth! Thou whose glory above the heavens is chanted by the mouths of babes and infants.

Psalm 8: 1, 2 NRSV

I do know what I want someone to give me for Christmas.
Wind-up mechanical toys
that make noises
and go round and round
and do funny things....
Well, okay, that's close, but not quite exactly it.
It's delight and simplicity that I want.
Foolishness and fantasy and noise.
Angels and miracles and wonder and innocence and magic.
That's closer to what I want.
It's harder to talk about,
but what I really, really want for Christmas is just this:
I want to be five years old again for an hour.[22]

O come, all ye faithful, joyful and triumphant;
O come ye, o come ye to Bethlehem;
Come and behold Him; born the King of angels;

Sing, choirs of angels, sing in exultation;
Sing all ye bright hosts of heaven above;
Glory to God, all glory in the highest.

Yea, Lord, we greet Thee, born this happy morning;
Jesus, to Thee be all glory given;
Word of the Father, now in flesh appearing.

O come, let us adore Him,
O come, let us adore Him,
O come let us adore Him,
Christ, the Lord.

Mary's humble acceptance of the divine will is the starting point of the story of redemption.

———◆●◆———

He has looked with favor on the lowliness of his servant.
Surely, from now on all generations will call me blessed.

Luke 1:48 NRSV

*A*s Joseph was a-walking
He heard an angel sing,
"This night shall be the birth-time
Of Christ, the Heavenly King.
"He neither shall be born
In house nor in hall,
Nor in a place of paradise,
But in an ox's stall.
"He shall not be clothed
In purple nor in pall;
But in the fair white linen,
That usen babies all.
"He neither shall be rocked
In silver nor in gold,
But in a wooden manger
That resteth on the mold."

The greatest gift you can share with a child is your good example of giving.

Don't let anyone look down on you because you are young,
but set an example for the believers
in speech, in life, in love, in faith, and in purity.

1 Timothy 4:12 NIV

A U.S. commander based in Bosnia at Christmas was distressed at the plight of the children.

He sent an e-mail message to fifty friends, with a holiday wish: please send supplies for the dilapidated schools of this war-torn corner of the world.

He had modest expectations for a few extra notebooks and some used toys.

Instead he was deluged when his fifty friends began contacting churches and more friends to trumpet his cause. Soon he and his men had delivered more than 600 boxes of clothes, toys, and supplies to the 30 schools in his region.

"It's going to be a wonderful Christmas," he said.[23]

Although the world is full of suffering,
it is full also of the overcoming of it.

Comfort ye my people.

Isaiah 40:1 KJV

I am not alone at all, I thought.

I *was never alone at all.*

And that, of course, is the message of Christmas.

We are never alone.

Not when the night is darkest, the wind coldest,
the world seemingly most indifferent.
For this is still the time God chooses.

Love is, above all, the gift of oneself.

God loves a cheerful giver.

2 Corinthians 9:7 NIV

*W*hat can I give him,
Poor as I am?

If I were a shepherd
I would bring a lamb.

If I were a Wise Man
I would do my part.

Yet what I can
I give him—

Give my heart.[24]

All you that to feasting
And mirth are inclined,
Come, here is Good News
For to pleasure your mind!

———◦•◦———

He who is of a merry heart has a continual feast.

Proverbs 15:15 NKJV

His country was in moral decline. Crime was rampant. Children were mistreated. And another evidence he noticed was that fewer and fewer people were celebrating Christmas traditions anymore.

Then he seized upon the idea for a story. He laughed and cried over the thought of it, as he wandered up to twenty miles a day up and down the streets of London, often into the wee hours of the night.

But just six weeks after he began writing this tale in October of 1843, Charles Dickens finished perhaps his best loved story: *A Christmas Carol*.

Dickens savored the Christmas spirit with a zest that year and hoped that others would follow his lead.[25]

Saying "I love you" is fine, but *showing* "I love you" is better.

———◆———

Since God so loved us, we also ought to love one another . . .
if we love one another, God lives in us
and his love is made complete in us.

I John 4: 11, 12 NIV

*P*robably the reason
we all go so haywire
at Christmastime,
with the endless, unrestrained,
and often silly
buying of gifts,
is that we don't quite know
how to put
our love into words.[26]

Joy to the world! The Lord is come!
Let earth receive her King;
let every heart prepare Him room,
And heaven and nature sing.

Joy to the earth the Savior reigns.
Let men their songs employ,
While fields and floods, rocks, hills and plains
repeat the sounding joy.

No more let sin and sorrows grow,
nor thorns infest the ground;
He comes to make His blessings flow
far as the curse is found.

He rules the world with truth and grace,
and makes the nations prove
The glories of His righteousness
and wonders of His love.

Eternal life and endless joy
are parts of the gift.

You will fill me with joy in your presence.

Psalm 16:11 NIV

*A*ll you who have a troubled heart,

listen to the angel's song:

"I bring you tidings of great joy!"

Jesus did not come to condemn you.

If you want to define Christ rightly,

then pay heed to how the angel defines him:

a great joy!

Let Christ radiate and live His life in you.
Let the poor, seeing you, be drawn to Christ
and invite Him to enter their homes and
their lives. Let the sick and suffering find in
you a real angel of comfort and consolation.

---

*Be imitators of God, therefore, as dearly loved children and
live a life of love, just as Christ loved us and gave himself
up for us as a fragrant offering and sacrifice to God.*

Ephesians 5:1, 2 NIV

Then let every heart keep Christmas within.

Christ's pity for sorrow,

Christ's hatred for sin,

Christ's care for the weakest,

Christ's courage for right.

Everywhere, everywhere, Christmas tonight![27]

O Christmas tree,
O Christmas tree,
Thy candles shine out brightly!

❦

The people living in darkness
have seen a great light.

Matthew 4:16 NIV

In the early 1900s, a young Denver boy who was sick asked his father to put lights on the big evergreen just outside his window. The boy's father, who operated an electrical business, strung colored lights on the evergreen. His son watched them sparkle like emeralds and rubies against their ermine mantle of snow.

In horse-drawn carriages and chugging automobiles, people came for miles around to admire the tree. The next year, neighbors joined in the outdoor tree-trimming.

It wasn't long before the lighted Christmas trees spread from home to home and became a holiday tradition. Today, in city parks, along highways, on dark and snow-drifted lawns alike, lighted living trees remind millions of the birth of Christ.

'Tis the gift to come down
where we ought to be
And when we find ourselves
in the place just right
'Twill be in the valley of love and delight.

*But seek first his kingdom and his righteousness,
and all these things will be given to you as well.*

Matthew 6:33 NRSV

Once a girl wished every day was Christmas. Much to her surprise and delight, her wish came true—endless presents, plenty of candy, and new toys to play with from dawn to dusk.

But after a week, she became quite cross, because she endured day after day of stomach aches, and every night she went to bed exhausted from all her playing and the endless excitement.

Her wish went on and on, past Valentine's Day. It didn't even skip April Fool's Day! Turkeys became scarce, selling for $1,000 apiece. One could trade a diamond for a cranberry. And when all the woods were cut down for Christmas trees, villagers made trees out of rags. By autumn, people didn't carry presents around nicely anymore. They flung them over the fence or through the window, and, instead of attaching loving notes to them, they started yelling, "Take it, you horrid old thing!"

Stripped of the spirit of Christmas and its true celebration of peace, joy, and goodwill to others, all the festivities were empty and burdensome, and most people became quite quarrelsome.

I always like the gifts I get,
But how I love the gifts I give!

———— ◆ ◆ ————

For all things come from Thee,
and from Thy hand we have given to Thee.

1 Chronicles 29:14 NAS

A pastor asked the church youth group to help a single mother who needed a car but could not afford one. He had found an inexpensive vehicle in good condition, and the youth group was to raise the funds. They had bake sales, car washes, and spaghetti dinners and even sponsored a "slave day," where the teens provided yardwork or housecleaning to parishioners for a donation.

On Christmas Eve, the single mother, who knew nothing of these efforts, answered her doorbell and found the entire youth group standing at her door. The young people sang, "We wish you a Merry Christmas," and one teen handed her the keys. Then the young people opened a path before her, and her eyes fell on the car she so desperately needed.

Years later, the young people still count that experience among their most memorable of all their teen-age activities. One young man said, "It was one time we really *did* something important for Christ for Christmas. I'll never forget it."

While shepherds kept their watching
o'er silent flocks by night,
Behold, throughout the heavens
there shone a holy light.

The shepherds feared and trembled
when lo! Above the earth
Rang out the angel chorus
that hailed our Savior's birth.

*Down in a lowly manger
the humble Christ was born,
And God sent us salvation
that blessed Christmas morn.*

*Go tell it on the mountain,
Over the hills and everywhere.
Go tell it on the mountain
That Jesus Christ is born!*

God has given us two hands
—one to receive with
and one to give with.
We are channels made for sharing.

———◆———

Give, and it will be given to you.
A good measure, pressed down, shaken together and
running over, will be poured into your lap.

Luke 6:38 NIV

Mrs. James selected a pretty design and "just-right" colors, buttons, and materials for a Christmas coat for her daughter. One morning, she paused from her knitting to gaze out at the snow, and a woman walked by. It was the young widow who lived nearby. Mrs. James couldn't help noticing the woman's old, threadbare coat as she shivered in the blustery weather. She was walking to her waitress job, and Mrs. James wondered how the widow managed to feed, clothe, and keep a roof over the heads of her six children.

All day, Mrs. James thought about the widow. By dusk, Mrs. James sewed on the last button and spotted the widow returning home from work. Tucking the coat into a box, she walked to the widow's door, laid down the package, rang the bell, and slipped quietly away. The next day, Mrs. James watched. Perhaps it was the big smile on her face or her beautiful new coat, but the young widow looked positively radiant.

Tomorrow I will knit a coat for my daughter, Mrs. James thought, *but this one was for my neighbor.* ❀

Peace! Peace! Jesus Christ was born to save.
Calls you one and calls you all
To gain his everlasting hall.

❖

Surely goodness and mercy
shall follow me all the days of my life:
and I will dwell in the house of the LORD forever.

Psalm 23:6 KJV

A U.S.A.F. sergeant in Thailand let his light shine. When others were out partying and chasing women, he stayed in, talked to other soldiers, relaxed, and read. A young soldier asked him why. The sergeant shared his faith in God with the young man and told him that his relationship with Jesus meant he made different lifestyle choices. The two began reading scriptures together and praying on a regular basis. The older soldier had the joy of leading the younger man to his Lord. Christmas was approaching, and the young man celebrated his new birth while the world celebrated Christ's birth.

Due to seniority, the sergeant went home for holiday leave, while others in the unit stayed behind. When he returned, the men in his unit met his plane with unhappy news. The young soldier had been killed in battle the day before.

Though deeply saddened by the passing of his young friend, the sergeant comforted the other soldiers with some good news: "This year, he really did get to go 'home' for Christmas."

Joy is the grace we say to God.

———◆•◆———

You will go out with joy,
and be led forth in peace.

Isaiah 55:12 NAS

*C*ompassionate and holy God,
we celebrate with joy your coming into our midst;
we celebrate with hope your coming into our midst;
we celebrate with peace your coming into our midst;
for you have come to save us.
By your grace we recognize your presence in men and women
in all parts of your world . . .
through your strength our lives can proclaim joy and hope;
through your love we can work for peace and justice.
You are the source of our being;
you are the light of our lives.

Christmas is a love affair
to remove the wrinkles
of the year.

———◆•◆———

*You loved me before the creation
of the world.*

John 17:24 NIV

*L*oving Father, help us remember the birth of Jesus,
that we may share in the song of the angels,
the gladness of the shepherds
and the wisdom of the wise men.
Close the door of hate
and open the door of love all over the world.
Let kindness come with every gift
and good desires with every greeting.
Deliver us from evil by the blessing which Christ brings
and teach us to be merry with clean hearts.
May the Christmas morning make us happy to be your children
and the Christmas evening bring us to our beds
with grateful thoughts, forgiving and forgiven,
for Jesus' sake. Amen.

A Christmas candle is
a lovely thing:
It makes no noise at all,
But softly gives itself away;
While quite unselfish, it grows small.

———————

The spirit of man is the candle of the LORD,
searching all the inward parts.

Proverbs 20:27 KJV

Residents of the small village of Beit Sahour light candles at dusk on Christmas, announcing their determination to keep the eternal message of peace alive.

Just east of Bethlehem, this is believed to be the village of the shepherds who heard the heavenly message, "peace on earth, good will among all."

In this troubled region of the world where strife dominates, the lighting of candles is a clear testimony that peace is only possible when we turn to the Babe in a Manger.[28]

O holy night,
the stars are brightly shining;
It is the night
of the dear Savior's birth!
Long lay the world
in sin and error pining,
Till He appeared
and the soul felt its worth.
A thrill of hope,
the weary soul rejoices,
For yonder breaks
a new and glorious morn.

Fall on your knees,

O hear the angel voices!

O night divine,

O night when Christ was born!

O night, O holy night,

O night divine!

Acknowledgments

Gerald Horton Bath (7), Mother Teresa (10,134), Gayle Edwards (11,21,27,141,147), John Greenleaf Whittier (13), Pipefuls (15), Taylor Caldwell (18,123), Rose Gallion (19,145), John Wesley (20), Charles Dickens (22,36,79), Phillips Brooks (23,135), A. F. Wells (24), Peter Marshall (25), Leo Tolstoy (26), Jennifer Gillia Costa (29), Jane Addams (32), Philip Sydney (34), Edward T. Sullivan (37), George MacDonald (38), Ruth Bell Graham (39), Walt Whitman (40), Sherry Morris (41,70,71), Walter Russell Bowie (44), Hendrick Willem Van Loon (45), Charles Wesley (46), Ian Hargreaver (47), John R. Rice (48), David Elkind (49), Mencius (50), Robert Murphy (51,93,109), Elie Wiesel (52), Marion Edey (53), Dorothy Grider (53), Catherine Hall (57), Cotvos (58), Harry Reasoner (59), Emerson (60), James S. Hewett (61,73,87), Ralph W. Sockman (62), Martin Luther (63,133), Robert Heinlein (64), Glenn Van Ekeren (65,89), Roy L. Smith (66), St. Ambrose of Milan (67), Richard Roberts (74), Howard Thurman (75), Billy Graham (76,144), Dale Evans Rogers (77), Washington Irving (78), W. C. Jones (84), Stephanie Goldberg (85), St. Irenaeus (86), Burton Hillis (88), Phillip Schaff (90), William Shakespeare (91), Guillaume Apollinaire (92), Theodore M. Hesburgh (96), Robert Browning (98), William Blake (99), Frances Frost (100), Erial Laborde (101), Helen Keller (102,122), Dick Bresnahan (105), Jeffrey Brian Michaels (110,128), Jim McDonough (111), Rubén Dario (113), Dr. Seuss (114), Robert Fulghum (115), Alan Richardson (118), Francis Balfour (120), Richard Newman (121), Jean Anouilh (124), Christina Rossetti (125), Geoffrez Rowell (127), Harlan Miller (129), Grady Johnson (137), William Dean Howells (139), Carolyn Wells (140), John M. Neale (146), Jean Ingelow (148), John Wanamaker (150), Robert Louis Stevenson (151), Eva K. Logue (152), Fred Strickert (153)

Endnotes

[1] *Encyclopedia of Religious Quotations,* Frank S. Mead (ed), (Grand Rapids, MI: Fleming H. Revell).

[2] *Illustrations Unlimited,* James Hewett (Wheaton, Ill: Tyndale House) 1988.

[3] *Ranger Rich,* December 1997.

[4] *Illustrations Unlimited,* James Hewett (Wheaton, Ill: Tyndale House) 1988.

[5] *Encyclopedia of Religious Quotations,* Frank S. Mead (ed), (Grand Rapids, MI: Fleming H. Revell).

[6] *New Statesman,* January 1998.

[7] *The Hurried Child* (Reading, MA: Addison-Wesley Longman) 1989.

[8] *Open the Door* (Charles Scribner's) 1949.

[9] *Holy Humor: A Book of Inspirational Wit* (New York: *Guideposts*) 1996.

[10] *Illustrations Unlimited,* James Hewett (Wheaton, Ill: Tyndale House) 1988.

[11] *Illustrations Unlimited,* James Hewett (Wheaton, Ill: Tyndale House) 1988.

[12] *The Speakers Sourcebook,* Glenn Van Ekeren (Prentice Hall) 1988.

[13] *Illustrations Unlimited,* James Hewett (Wheaton, Ill: Tyndale House) 1988.

[14] *The Work of Christmas,* Howard Thurman.

[15] *Encyclopedia of Religious Quotations,* Frank S. Mead (ed), (Grand Rapids, MI: Fleming H. Revell).

[16] *Ladies Home Journal,* December 1997.

[17] *Illustrations Unlimited,* James Hewett (Wheaton, Ill: Tyndale House) 1988.

[18] *The Speakers Sourcebook,* Glenn Van Ekeren (Prentice Hall) 1988.

[19] *New Orleans Magazine,* December 1997.

[20] *America,* January 1998.

[21] *Holy Humor: A Book of Inspirational Wit* (New York: *Guideposts*) 1996.

[22] *All I Really Need to Know I Learned in Kindergarten,* Robert Fulghum (New York: Ballantine), 1989.

[23] *US News and World Report,* December 1997.

[24] *A Christmas Feast,* Edna Barth (ed), (Boston: Houghton Mifflin).

[25] *History Today,* December 1993.

[26] *Encyclopedia of Religious Quotations,* Frank S. Mead (ed), (Grand Rapids, MI: Fleming H. Revell).

[27] *Encyclopedia of Religious Quotations,* Frank S. Mead (ed), (Grand Rapids, MI: Fleming H. Revell).

[28] *The Tenth Century,* December 1997.

Additional copies of this book and other titles in the Honor Books Christmas series are available from your local bookstore.

The Living Nativity, by David & Helen Haidle
The Wonder of Christmas, by Derric Johnson
God's Little Christmas Book, portable
A Treasury of Christmas Classics, clothbound
The Greatest Christmas Ever, clothbound gift edition
The Greatest Christmas Ever, portable
The Candymaker's Gift, by David & Helen Haidle
The Indescribable Gift, by Richard Exley *
Christmas Treasures of the Heart, by Cheri Fuller
Straight from the Heart for Christmas, by Richard Exley

Honor Books
Tulsa, Oklahoma